Coachi…
and custome… …ce
success

Fullbrook, Heslop,
Morden and Sellwood

Published by Prosell Learning Limited

ISBN Number 978-0-9928851-0-6

Contents

Preface

Performance coaching and our journey

The roots of performance coaching

Performance coaching has been around for centuries: Socrates and Aristole wrote about motivation, learning and performance some 2,000 years ago. Today, in education, sport and in the workplace these themes are just as relevant. Teachers, sports coaches and managers bear a great responsibility both as coaches and leaders. What they do and how they behave impacts on an individual's motivation, skill, performance and personal growth.

Where did we start?

For us, our understanding of the benefits of performance coaching in the workplace started in the early eighties. We were working as Operational Managers responsible for Call Centre, Field Sales and Customer Service teams – and were keen for our staff to deliver consistent levels of outstanding performance.

The importance of implementing processes, with measurable objectives, was clearly understood. We analysed and fine-tuned methods of measurement, renumeration, working conditions, individual profiling and recruitment. And naturally, we relied heavily on training to instill effective working practices.

However, despite some early success, material, long lasting improvements in performance eluded us. Academic research supported our experiences – training alone does not result in sustained change. So what would? To have a real impact on the bottom line, it became clear that we would have to focus on the manager's role in supporting an individual's change in performance.

Procoach Performance coaching

We have embedded this practical know-how into our Procoach performance coaching model. It has taken many years to refine and is based on in-depth knowledge about what really works. Our trainers, coaches and customers have provided invaluable feedback, generously sharing their insights with us. We have measured the impact of the Procoach model across a range of key performance indicators. Excitingly, it delivers the type of results that we were seeking back in the eighties.

What is different about Procoach?

The Procoach model helps mangers become world-class performance coaches. While many organisations offer performance coaching, not all ensure that managers can use these skills in the workplace, with different individuals across a range of roles.

Rather than one-off training events, at Prosell, we believe that managers will benefit most from direct learning support in their workplace. Our approach is to observe and develop managers while they work with their teams. We refresh and enhance their skills each year, with a workplace review and further coaching skill development.

What skills do we introduce to managers?

We introduce skills that deliver business results and maximise any investment in training, recruitment and remuneration. These skills are both about what to do and how to go about it.

We give managers the confidence to encourage the best performance from every individual. They learn to performance coach, to improve ability and motivation:

- Using a balance of directive and non-directive coaching styles, to suit the individual coachee
- In impromptu and formal situations

We help managers to appreciate that performance coaching takes multiple conversations. Using Procoach, managers provide a stretching and supportive environment. They set expectations, measure performance, coach ability and motivation issues. They also discuss feedback, evaluate successes and development opportunities.

A workplace with these elements means you have engaged employees who are likely to be loyal to the organisation, reducing attrition rates. They in turn will be motivated to provide a good service to your customers. This increases retention and referrals – leading to greater profits. This is the concept of the Service-Profit Chain (James L. Heskett, 2008).

Remember – engaged employees results in greater profits!

Where are we now?

Despite the research and our personal experiences about what works, organisations still invest millions in classroom training that they do not follow up through coaching, practice or measurement.

We continue to challenge organisations to recognise and act on what we know and what the research confirms. We talk to them about the influence of workplace activities on performance. And we encourage them to look beyond traditional classroom based skills training to consider the impact of managers on customer facing teams and their performance.

We will continue to shape Procoach to reflect the best, most current research and practical insights we experience. And we will persist in encouraging organisations to invest in effective development approaches.

We have written this book to share what we have developed with people who want to have a sustained impact on performance through individuals and teams.

When reading this book...

It is easy for us to claim successes in many types of organisation, but you may need to be convinced that our approach will fit with your specific organisational requirements.

We ask that you read about our approach in this book, and try it. Then please give us some feedback; we would like to know what you think of our Procoach approach in relation to your organisation. And we can continue to share the collective experiences of how organisations effectively improve the performance of their people.

Simon Morden
CEO, Prosell Learning Limited

Acknowledgements

Thanks are due to all of our customers, coaches, trainers and business partners who have contributed greatly to the content and deployment of the Procoach approach.

Special mention must go to two people. Firstly Rachel Auckland for her support in the writing and launching of this book. Secondly to Hajar De Chausay who did so much to help shape the content with us in the early days.

Chapter 1

Striving for sustained performance improvement

What drives continuous performance improvement?

Introduction

> "The greater danger for most of us lies not in setting our aim too high and falling short, but in setting our aim too low, and achieving our mark."
>
> MICHELANGELO

Key chapter points

- What to consider when trying to close a 'performance gap'.
- Who, aside from the individual, has the greatest influence on a 'performance gap' or 'performance potential'.
- What the performance coach can do to create an environment where an individual's performance can prosper.

In this chapter we consider three areas that impact performance, placing performance coaching in a business context.

In the next chapter we take a detailed look at Procoach, Prosell's approach to performance improvement. We explain how it works and why it has such an impact on an individual's ability to improve their performance.

1. Components that define individual performance

During our journey we sought to understand what influences an individual's performance. We identified three internal components:

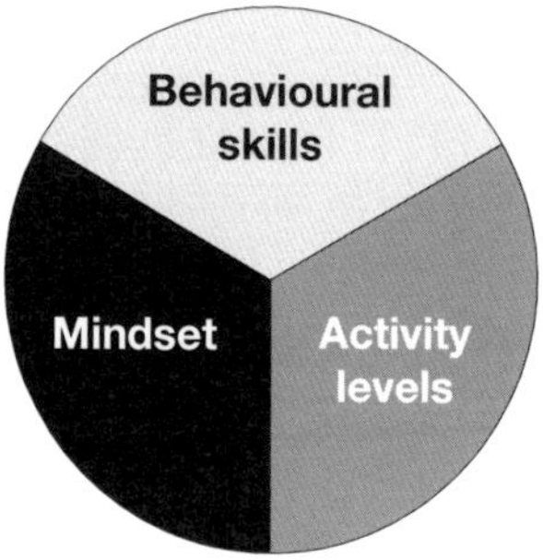

These components impact performance individually and collectively.

Mindset	Why we do something and our commitment to doing it.
Behavioural skills	How well we do something.
Activity levels	How often we do something.

2. The greatest external influences for reducing a performance gap

Naturally individuals do not work in isolation. Other influences affect performance such as resources available i.e. the tools for the job, time and budget.

We have based our conclusions about which have the greatest external impact by referencing research and our own 30 years of business experiences. We have found that line managers have the biggest influence on someone's motivation and performance levels.

You'll find brief details about this research, carried out by the Sales Executive Council, Prosell's own research and Service Profit Chain, at the end of this book.

3. Important beliefs and actions for a performance coach

An effective performance coach creates an environment in which an individual's performance can prosper. Their ability to do this depends on their actions and beliefs.

Procoach helps managers to become world class performance coaches. We see their role as:

"Maximising the performance of an individual, by helping them explore, challenge and develop their skill and commitment levels."

We achieve this through awareness, practice and feedback in the workplace.

Our question

What can performance coaches do in order to deliver continuous performance improvement?

We will answer this question in detail in the next chapter when we complete our summary of Procoach.

First we introduce you to **David**, a line manager and **Emma**, his new team member. They will be taking this journey with you.

Case Study

Emma joins David's team:

Emma has been working in David's team for two weeks.

She has already noticed that David and the rest of the team communicate in a different way, compared to her previous experiences.

In particular she has noted that:

1. She has already discussed her role with David and is clear about her contribution to the team and how they collectively support the business.

2. David and the team acknowledge exceptional work. Only yesterday David made a point of congratulating a colleague, Tony for his thorough analysis of a competitor's products.

3. David encourages and listens to ideas put forward by the team. Emma understands that he's adopted many of their ideas in the past.

4. Regular one-to-one meetings take place with David. She is due to discuss the highs and lows of her first two weeks, the next day.

Emma concludes that David and the team work well together and everyone in the team is prepared to go the extra mile, because they feel valued.

Chapter check

What have you learnt from this chapter?

Check your knowledge by answering these questions:

Self assessment questions

1. Which three internal componants have we identified, that influence an individual's performance?
2. Who represents the greatest external influence on an individual's performance?
3. What does a performance coach need to do to help performance prosper?

Chapter 1 – Summary & Actions

In this chapter we examined the:

- Influences affecting individual performance
- Components that determine an individual's performance
- The greatest external influence on performance.
- Role of the performance coach in improving individual performance

Your action plan

Consider the actions you will take to encourage performance improvement in your team, department or company.

Ask yourself:

- How am I currently encouraging and supporting performance improvement in your team?
- How does my team rate in terms of their desire and skills to support performance improvement?
- What management structure and processes are in place to encourage a performance coaching climate?

Make a note of any aspects that you feel you can improve. Then plan how to make a start on the areas you have identified. Finally read the following case study about Emma's progress before moving onto the next chapter.

Case Study

Emma experiences the performance improvement cycle:

Emma has now worked in David's team for a month.

In that time she has had a number of impromptu performance discussions with David. Many of these take no more than five minutes; they have been useful in resolving particular difficulties Emma has faced. These discussions help Emma as she can immediately put into action the ideas they discuss.

Emma is about to have her first formal review. She arrives at the meeting with some notes about her performance. David suggested that she refresh her memory of the key performance indicators (KPIs) required of her role and asked that she also review some of the projects she's worked on so far, to see how they measure up against the KPIs.

During the meeting Emma and David have an open discussion about how she is performing. They agree on how Emma's current skill levels measure up against the KPIs. Emma is pleased that David is listening to her assessment although he challenges a particularly negative view Emma has of one aspect of her performance, reinforcing his comments with data that he has collected.

Overall Emma believes she has progressed well and David agrees, commenting that Emma has picked up key parts of her role quickly.

Before concluding the meeting, David asks Emma to complete a summary of the areas on which they have agreed she will work and corresponding actions.

They agree to meet again in a month to review progress and David reminds Emma that she should continue to ask for help as she needs it.

Chapter 2

Prosell's performance improvement approach

An overview of Prosell's Procoach programme

Introduction

"Coaching is unblocking a person's potential to maximise their own performance. It is helping them to learn, rather than to teach them."

TIMOTHY GALLWEY

Key chapter points

- Summarise the Procoach Model of performance development.
- Identify why an individual may have development needs.
- Outline the components that comprise the Procoach programme.

DEFINITION

Procoach:
An effective coaching approach which delivers continuous performance improvement.

We have created this programme by building on the experience of our customers, coaching experts and coachees.

So far we have considered the importance of performance improvement, the influences on individual development and growth and the components that contribute to performance.

This chapter introduces the Procoach model, the result of nearly 30 years of experience of working with sales and customer service teams around the world.

In the following chapter we examine the rationale and principles that form the basis of Procoach. In later chapters we specifically move onto a detailed examination of the Procoach model and how, with some key coaching tools, this provides an effective approach to continuous performance improvement.

Procoach for performance improvement coaching

Prosell's performance improvement approach, Procoach, is a robust performance coaching methodology that allows managers to continuously develop the capabilities of people within their team.

Procoach is centred on our A-E model. We explain what happens at each of the model's five steps in more detail in later chapters.

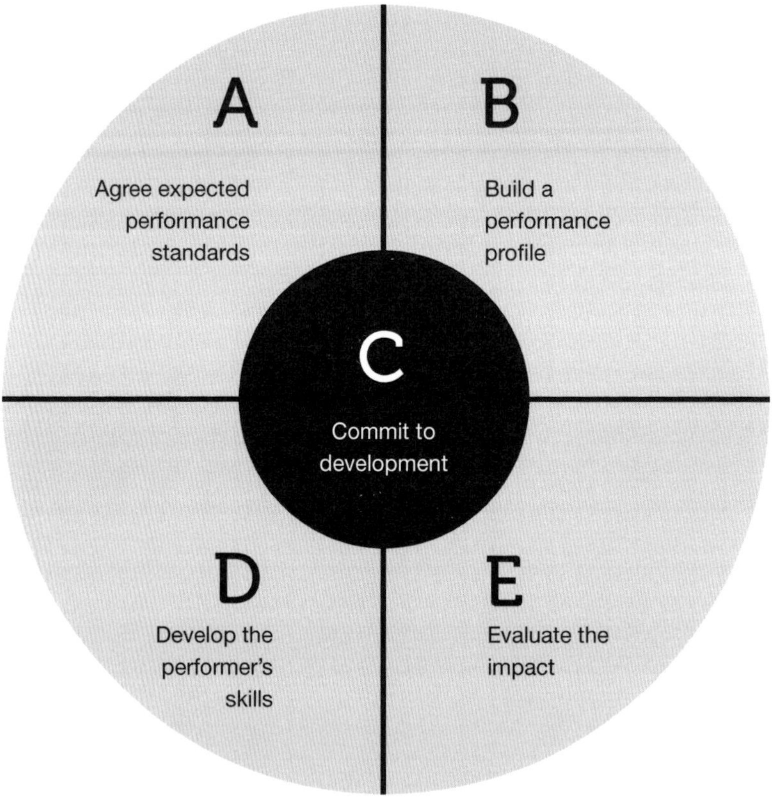

"Faith is taking the first step even when you can't see the whole staircase."

MARTIN LUTHER KING JR.

Performance gaps and coachee potential

In a business context, we describe performance gaps as the difference between an individual's current performance and what is required of them. This creates an opportunity to build on an individual's current performance.

Expectations of an individual will change as experience in the role grows – so performance gaps need to be continually monitored.

Performance gaps might result from a need to develop a skill, improve motivation or increase activity levels.

Prosell's Procoach approach helps coaches identify the underlying cause of a performance gap and provides a means of:

Case Study

Emma receives support during her attempts to work on a performance gap:

Emma has now been with David's team for three months.

She is progressing well and is delighted with the positive comments both David and her colleagues have made.

At their monthly catch up David asked how she was coping with the increasing need to write reports. Emma is pleased that David raised this question, as she recently took on a responsibility to prepare and distribute a weekly report to several departments. Emma receives a lot of calls about the report, impacting the time she now has available for other tasks.

Emma explains the issue and David acknowledges that he has noticed this also. He asks "What do you think is the reason for these calls?".

Emma is unsure but after some discussion she concludes that the callers are looking for clarification about how she reached conclusions rather than questioning the validity of her data. She explains to David that she has been writing the report as best she can, but struggles to explain in a logical sequence how she has used her data to reach a conclusion.

Next David asks what could help improve her report structure. Emma thinks for a moment and then suggests she talks with Jan, a team colleague. She has noticed that Jan has a 'way with words' and Emma already turns to her for a phrase or description. David agrees this is a good idea. Emma agrees to arrange a formal session with Jan, to help her present her thoughts in a more structured way.

Emma promises to put any tips from Jan into action and let David know about her progress.

Effective performance improvement

Within our Procoach Programme we place emphasis on:

"What to coach"

DEFINITION

What to coach
The skills and processes needed by individuals to produce outstanding performance.

"Analytical Skills"

DEFINITION

Analytical Skills
The diagnostic skills of the coach applied to specific information /data in any given situation.

"How to coach"

DEFINITION

How to coach
The actions a coach take that bring about effective behavioral change.

"Never, never, never give up."
WINSTON CHURCHILL

Tangible, continuous results through coaching excellence

Our Procoach programme has a clear focus on tangible and continuous performance results. It is not just about the coaching conversation, it is about incorporating and embracing all facets of performance development and continuous improvement.

We believe that any development programme should have at its core a method by which learners can transfer their newly developed skills into their workplace. We therefore combine development of skills and processes with workplace support and reinforcement.

We also set out the standards that participants will achieve in order to be certified at the end of the programme. We ask participants to provide evidence during the programme to show they have reached these standards, to achieve certification.

We implement Procoach in partnership with our customers, reinforcing skills through development activities such as practice and feedback. We encourage the coach to review their skill and knowledge levels once they have completed each scheduled part of the programme.

This helps participants to make incremental adjustments to their approach as necessary. We support this approach through an annual re-certification to check that each coach continues to deliver coaching, which is effective and impactful.

During our Procoach programme we integrate processes with skills. This ensures that as participants build their competence, it is evident to them what to do and when. Beyond the foundation programme, as they progress to different levels, the emphasis shifts to building an appreciation of how to develop intuitive and instinctive forms of performance coaching.

Skills for effective performance coaching

Procoach ensures participants possess the skills they need to identify gaps and blocks to an individual's working practice.

In some instances it will be skills or knowledge, in other instances it will be attitude or motivation. Procoach gives the participant the skills and confidence to handle any given situation.

In the following chapters we look at how we achieve this.

Case Study

David reflects on his performance coaching experience:

Although initially sceptical of its impact, David has been putting performance coaching into practice for almost a year.

With a formal re-certification looming, he is keen to evaluate how he has progressed in helping his team grow. He is also interested in assessing the business results he has observed.

David acknowledged to himself that he was pleased with the way he had coached Emma so far. It was the first opportunity he had had to coach someone new to the team. He felt that he had built rapport quickly and that Emma was relaxed during their review meetings.

He thought back to his recent meeting with Emma. How had that impacted her growth and the business results?

Well, he had uncovered the cause of the difficulties she had with report writing. He had been particularly pleased that the questions he had asked helped Emma to reach her own conclusions. He had been tempted to jump in and offer his own ideas all too often in the past. Not too bad on the coaching front then.

David recognised his own limitations though, and he knew that Jan was far better at structuring reports than he was. It was a good decision to ask Jan to support Emma with this, after all he could not be an expert at everything. He would have to make sure she knew what Emma needed of course, but Jan was great at coaching other team members, he was sure she would help Emma.

When Emma's report writing skills improved, it made a real difference to her productivity and confidence. Together with the time saved by the teams who were currently questioning Emma's reports, David reckoned this resulted in increased efficiency and improved profitability for the company.

He would have to quantify the impact when Emma began to take on more work.

Chapter check

What have you learnt in this chapter?

Check your knowledge by answering these questions:

Self assessment questions

1. How would you define the purpose of the Procoach approach?
2. Which model is at the centre of the Procoach approach?
3. What steps are used as part of our Procoach approach to reinforce and support the learning?

Chapter 2 – Summary & Actions

In this chapter we:

- Summarised the Procoach Model of performance development
- Identified why an individual may have development needs
- Outlined the components and elements that comprise the Procoach programme

Your action plan

Consider the actions you will take to encourage performance improvement in your team, department or company.

Ask yourself:

- How am I currently facilitating performance development?
- What causes do I typically identify for these development needs?

Make a note of any aspects that you feel you can improve. Then plan how to make a start on the areas you've identified.

Chapter 3

Principles, skills and our model

The foundation of Procoach

Procoach: our reasons for this approach

"Always make a total effort, even when the odds are against you."

ARNOLD PALMER

Key chapter points

- The values that underpin effective performance coaching.
- The need for a coaching mindset to create optimum conditions for coaching.
- Observable behavioural skills we recommend as a Procoach tool.

Performance driven

People evaluate and measure coaching by different indicators and methods, and this can be because of the different problems coaching looks to tackle. At Prosell we believe that coaching is only effective if it delivers improved performance. We develop coaches who can bring out the best in their people and contribute to the results of the business and team they represent.

Performance Results

At the heart of Procoach is a set of foundations, which we believe make the difference between a good and great performance coaching experience. Understanding the rationale behind the programme's design will help you identify how Procoach can benefit you.

The five foundations of the Procoach approach are:

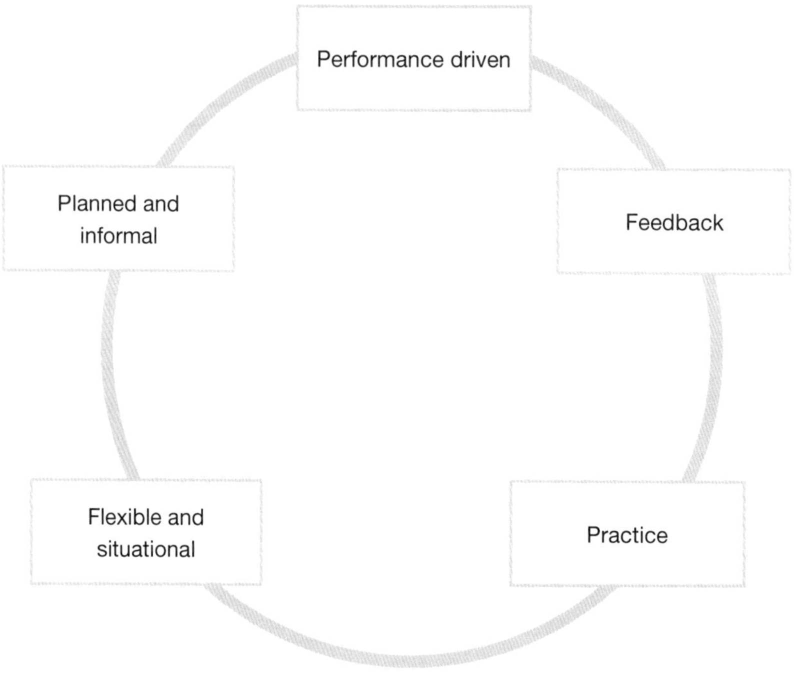

Explaining our values

Performance driven

A coach taking a successful performance-driven approach places an emphasis on measuring their coachee's behaviours, working practices and performance results. With appropriate support from their coach, coachees are engaged in analysing their performance and creating their own self-administered development plans. Depending on the circumstances, it may be necessary to challenge the coachee to help them acknowledge or build awareness of improvement opportunities.

Feedback

To develop their working practice, a coachee needs to be aware of what they are doing and why. Without effective feedback this is virtually impossible; enhancing self awareness, through feedback, is the precursor to development.

Effective performance improvement coaching involves the coachee analysing their performance. The coachee should then discuss their conclusions with their coach in an open and candid conversation.

Practice

To improve skills in the workplace, there is no substitute for practice. Procoach uses a specific coaching approach to help the coachee learn or refresh skills based on prior experience, or modelling others.

Our experience of coachees from different organisational backgrounds has convinced us that an effective environment is one where the coachee is able to practice in a risk free environment. The importance of disciplined, challenging practice as an essential component of success ("it must be lived and learned") is confirmed in research carried out by other writers in this field (Syed, 2011).

"For every failure, there's an alternative course of action. You just have to find it. When you come to a roadblock, take a detour."

MARY KAY ASH

Flexible and situational

We believe that an effective coaching experience is one where the coach alters their approach to reflect the capability, experience and attitude of the coachee. For example if the coachee is very motivated, knowledgeable and skilled, the coach will adopt a more hands-off style. This will involve more asking rather than telling the coachee how to do things.

If coaching is flexible and situational you would expect to see a coachee who is very engaged in the conversation or practice.

In terms of recognising the type of coaching needed, we recommend that the coach discuss how the coachee wants to be coached from the outset to identify the optimum "coaching" approach.

Planned and informal

Effective performance coaching can be both planned and informal. We designed our Procoach approach for use in both situations. You can use it effectively during a formal performance review and development process and during a spontaneous "do you have a minute..." coaching conversation.

In both cases, the coach would help the coachee identify areas of performance potential, or where it is possible to enhance existing good practice. They then use Procoach behaviours to address the situation.

The precise method of introducing a coaching approach into an organisation will depend on the nature of the business. Procoach has delivered continuous, tangible performance results in a cross section of business types, markets and countries.

"We first make our habits, and then our habits make us."

JOHN DRYDEN

An optimum coaching mindset

In Chapter 1 we introduced the idea of a coachee's mindset. We contend that a coachee needs a growth mindset to provide the optimum conditions for performance improvement. It is equally important for a coach to adopt a coaching mindset; one that provides the coachee with the most advantageous environment in which to grow.

As part of the Procoach programme, we introduce these principles:

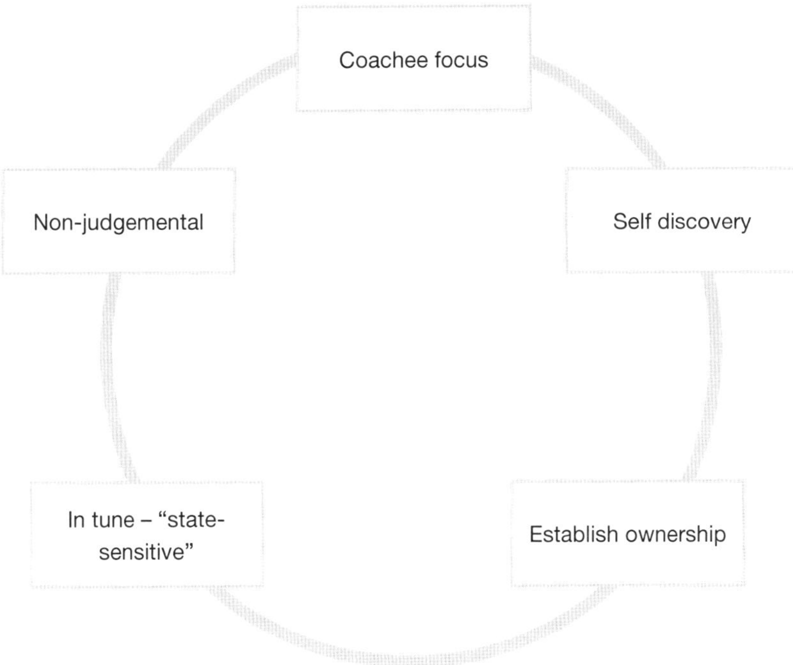

We believe that a coach can be highly effective if they are able to apply these principles to the coaching situations they encounter and therefore adopt an effective mindset.

The Procoach principles: defined

Here is a description of the Procoach principles and examples of how to recognise if they are being applied.

1. Coachee focus

What it means	The focus is on the coachee and their needs. This increases the chances of the coachee being engaged and maximising their potential.
What you would look for	The coach will constantly engage, support and involve the coachee. Look for eye contact, verbal nods and other physical signs of giving attention to the coachee.

2. Self discovery

What it means	The coachee is encouraged to participate, to increase their awareness of their performance, the reasons and their options to develop or enhance their working practice. The coachee physically and emotionally experiences the learning.
What you would look for	Coaching discussions or practical skills coaching where the emphasis is on asking the coachee to do or discover something. For example, a coach might ask a coachee to think about the impact of their behaviour, or to come up with ideas based on their experience. In practical skills coaching, this often involves the coachee in practice and feedback exchange.

3. Establish ownership

What it means	An environment is created in which the coachee takes ownership for their development.
What you would look for	The coachee will suggest where they need support. The coachee will also be self aware of their skill, knowledge and motivation levels.

4. In tune – "state sensitive"

What it means	The coach is 'in the moment' with the coachee's current state. The coach uses different behaviours to engage the coachee effectively.
What you would look for	The coach will use similar language and check that the activity has benefited the coachee. The coach and the coachee might also mirror body language and use similar words.

5. Non-judgemental

What it means	Building trust means the coachee can express themselves freely. This creates a learning environment in which a coachee shares ideas, makes discoveries about themselves and practices skills without fear of judgement.
What you would look for	The coach asks questions which are non-directive. Their questions and responses demonstrate acceptance and support of the coachee irrespective of what they say or do. They will seek to understand the coachee's beliefs and concerns by exploring the topic, rather than jumping to conclusions.

Case Study

David reviews his coaching mindset:

Looking back at his performance review meeting with Emma, David decides to examine his mindset and evaluate whether he is measuring up as a coach.

He considers each of the mindset principles in turn.

Coachee focus: David is confident that he had coached with Emma's best interests in mind. Although he initiated the discussion about her reports, Emma recognised that she was struggling.

Self discovery: Emma struggled to identify the cause of her challenges at first, but David was pleased that his questions helped her reach her own conclusions about the help she needed.

Establish ownership: During the conversation David was pleased to observe that Emma felt a responsibility to improve her report writing skills. So he focussed his attention on helping Emma arrive at a solution that would work for her; spending some time with Jan.

In tune, "state sensitive": Emma had been ready for an open discussion about her performance on this occasion. David felt he'd responded in kind, acknowledging her comments about the number of calls she was receiving from other teams and confirming her concerns were something that she needed to address.

Non judgemental: David worked hard in earlier discussions with Emma to help her become less cautious when discussing performance gaps. The most recent discussion showed that this caution had disappeared; David had been able to respond with more questions and feedback about the difficulties she had faced than when they started.

"You can't cross the sea merely by standing and staring at the water."

RABINDRANATH TAGORE

Chapter check

What have you learnt from this chapter?

In this chapter we described the foundations of our Procoach programme and some of the skills that support our approach to performance improvement.

Check your knowledge by answering these questions:

Self assessment questions

1. What are the values of the Procoach approach?
2. What mindset does a coach need, to allow them to carry out effective performance improvement coaching?

Chapter 3 – Summary & Actions

In this chapter we examined the:

- Values that underpin great performance coaching
- Benefits of a coaching mindset creating optimum conditions for coaching

Your action plan

Consider the actions you will take to encourage performance improvement in your team, department or company.

Ask yourself:

- Which of the values we have described in this chapter can you relate to? Which might you wish to work on?
- How appropriate is my mindset when I am coaching others?

Make a note of any aspects that you feel you can improve. Then plan how to make a start on the areas you've identified.

"Alone we can do so little; together we can do so much."

HELEN KELLER

The Procoach A-E model

Bringing about change in an organisation can take some effort. Your attempts to change and grow may be met with indifference, or even active disagreement. The benefits however are significant. Imagine what you could achieve if you persevere in your efforts to adopt best practice coaching into your organisation. What difference could it make to you, your team and your organisation?

In the following chapters we examine the Procoach A-E model in more depth. This model provides a framework through which to structure effective coaching.

In this framework, we offer additional tips to putting performance coaching into action, demonstrating how you can use the tools we examined in the last chapter via this framework.

After reading these chapters and the supporting information we've already introduced, consider how you can use the concepts described to effect change and grow as an individual.

The Procoach A-E model

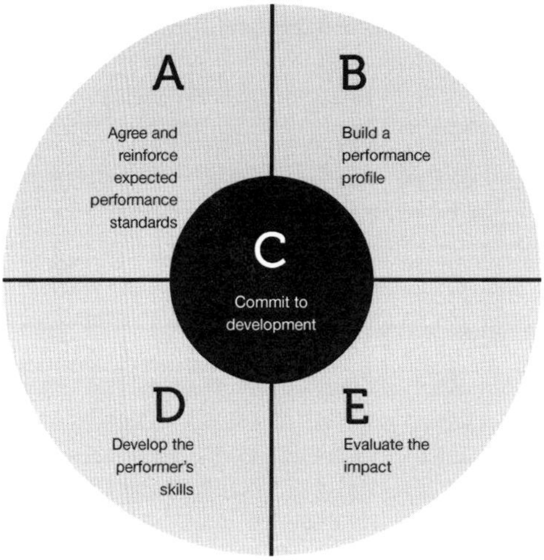

Chapter 4

Step A of Procoach: Agree Expected Performance Standards

"The choice to be excellent begins with aligning your thoughts and words with the intention to require more from yourself."

OPRAH

A: Agree expected performance standards

Key chapter points

- Agree with your coachee what is expected, so that they are clear what is required of them.
- Have regular discussions about performance standards to reflect your coachee's developing skills.
- Include both qualitative and quantitative measures, when agreeing performance standards.

The starting point for our description of the Procoach A-E model, as you might expect, is Step A.

During this step of the Procoach process you define and agree with a coachee what performance standards are required of them. If a role description exists this might form part of your discussion, to communicate and ensure each coachee understands what is expected of them.

It is important to note that although we are describing Step A as the starting point, this is for ease of description. In practice your focus on Step A doesn't just take place when you first start to coach a member of your team. Instead you would expect to communicate on a regular and ongoing basis, the standards expected of your coachee as they continuously enhance their working practice. These standards might change over time, so you might find it sufficient to reinforce some standards. Others may need to be updated – needing a discussion and agreement with your coachee.

Performance standards for high performing individuals

There are two key elements to setting performance standards. You need to define, communicate and gain commitment to both of these if you want to develop a high performing coachee.

We refer to these elements as the Qual/Quan mix. They include both qualitative and quantitative performance standards, relating to a coachee's role.

Job Role
Normally captured in a job description this describes the scope of their responsibilities

Used to agree

Performance standards
Quality and quantity

- The ***qualitative*** standards (skills and knowledge), that define expected working practice.
- The ***quantitative*** standards (normally expressed as KPIs and personal targets/objectives) that describe what performance or activity levels you expect someone to achieve.

These elements will have to be demonstrably fair, achievable and capable of measurement for a coachee to commit to them.

Your role as a performance coach in setting expectations

As a performance coach you would:

- Address any questions or concerns the coachee has about their expected performance.
- Agree with your coachee the performance standards required of them that:
    - include qualitative and quantitative standards.
    - show objective results.
    - are linked to business goals.

Although expectations of someone's performance standards will be specific to the individual, we've included some examples here of areas that would potentially be included.

Performance expectations: Sales Consultant

Performance area	Example performance measure
Achieve agreed targets and objectives	Achieve a pipeline to conversion rate of 50%
Meet customer centred key performance indicators	All new enquiries to be directed to the correct team within 2 minutes
Demonstrate an agreed call quality level, the structure and behaviours used	Customer needs identified correctly in 95% of calls

Performance expectations: Project Manager

Performance area	Example performance measure
Meet project deadlines, and financial targets	Project margin to be within 5% of that estimated at project start
Handle expected project volumes	Able to manage up to 4 projects without causing project delays
Demonstrate quality within all written and spoken communications	Instructions to project personnel re-clarified in no more than 10% of cases

Case Study

David examines how he approached Step A with Emma:

Having reviewed his coaching techniques, David decides to make some notes about how he has used the Procoach A-E process with Emma, since she joined the team.

- Job role: yes, he had given her the standard job description for her role. They had discussed a couple of points on it and Emma was happy with the content.

- Performance standards: in Emma's case, David had discussed Emma's performance during their monthly reviews and they had jointly agreed some performance goals that helped her contribute to the team's targets. They had agreed some deadlines and also the standard expected of Emma for each of the goals. David had also given Emma the opportunity to discuss how her role and the team's goals fitted into the company's wider strategic direction. Therefore she was aware of how her contribution made a difference to business profitability.

Chapter check

What have you learnt from this chapter?

Check your knowledge by answering these questions:

Self assessment questions

1. What is the purpose of Step A of Procoach?

2. Which two elements do you need to define, communicate and gain commitment to, when agreeing performance expectations?

3. What is your role as a coach, within Step A of Procoach?

Chapter 4 – Summary & Actions

In this chapter we suggested that you should:

- Agree with your coachee what is expected, so they are clear about what is required of them
- Have regular, ongoing discussions about performance standards to reflect your coachee's developing skills
- Include both qualitative and quantitative measures, when agreeing performance standards

Your action plan

Consider the actions you will take to encourage performance improvement in your team, department or company.

Ask yourself:

- Do your team members know what is expected of them currently? Are there any areas that you could clarify for each of them?
- How often do you discuss performance standards with your coachees? Is this sufficient?
- What measures are currently in place to measure performance standards? Are these both qualitative and quantitative?

Chapter 5

Step B of Procoach: Build a performance profile

B: Build a performance profile

Key chapter points

- Draw on a number of sources to identify your coachee's current performance profile.
- Examine both quantitative and qualitative measures of performance to obtain a rounded view of performance.
- Collect data and encourage your coachee to do this also.
- Analyse performance objectively – using indicators such as KPIs to determine whether an individual's current performance standards will enable you to achieve your team's business objectives.

As we discussed at the beginning of Chapter 2, to help your coachee grow in their role, you need to understand where they can make improvements. This might be between their agreed performance standards goal and their current level of performance.

Or, if the coachee is already performing at the level required of their role, it might be that there is "coachee potential". This is the performance potential that you know or suspect your coachee is capable of achieving.

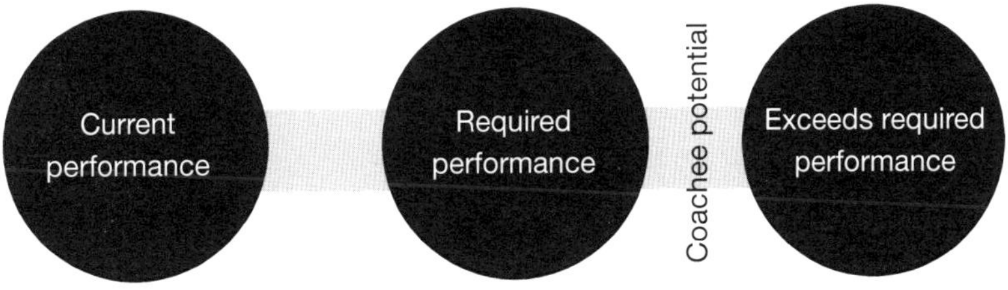

Performance analysis options

You can analyse performance gaps and the coachee's potential using both quantitative and qualitative evidence.

Quantitative:	**Qualitative:**
• Performance goals e.g. targets • Achievement of deadlines, internal or customer driven • Number of customer complaints	• Customer or peer feedback • Direct skill observation • Requests for re-work / correction

There are a variety of ways you can obtain quantitative and qualitative information to form a profile of the coachee. For example you could:

- Use management information from your records or systems.
- Use questions to check a coachee's knowledge levels.
- Observe the coachee performing a task.
- Ask the coachee to explain how they would currently complete specific tasks.

Having completed this analysis and encouraged your coachee to do the same, you can decide on the focus areas. You can then discuss with your coachee the opportunities, to enhance their performance.

Comparing current and required performance

When analysing performance, it is important to carry out an objective measurement.

Typically businesses use metrics to signpost whether they will achieve business results. You will no doubt have measures such as these, in your own organisation. For example, your sales team might measure pipeline size, value or mix to determine the expected revenue. Metrics are therefore indicators of current performance, compared to that required.

1. Your analysis of activity and the Qual/Quan mix will help you form a view of your coachee's working practice.
2. You can then determine whether their efforts are likely to be sufficiently close to the required standard by checking whether your team are likely to achieve their KPIs.
3. If they are, it is a good indicator that they will meet business targets. If not, you will need to examine the gaps in knowledge, skill and/or behavior that require your attention to close the gap.

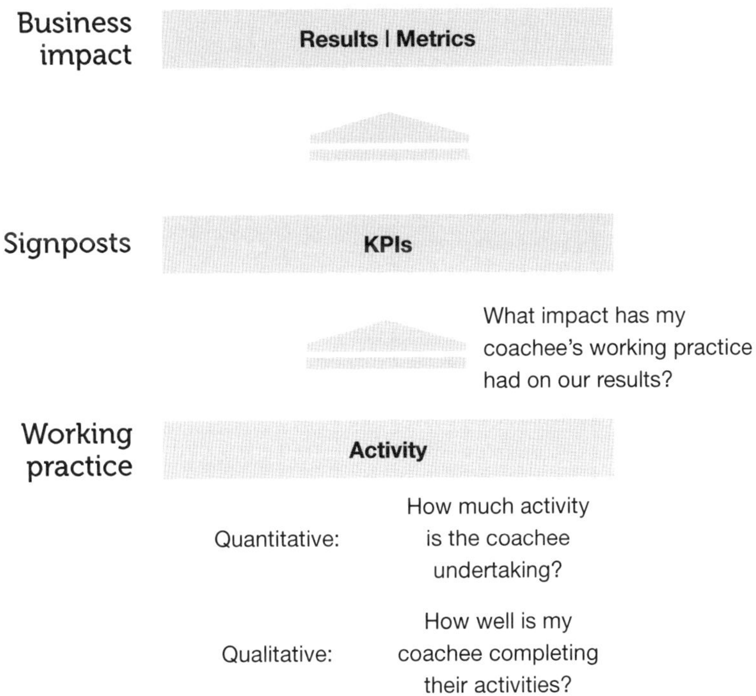

Case Study

David examines how he approached Step B with Emma:

David moves onto an examination of his approach to Step B. Their recent discussion about report writing helps here.

He reminds himself of the relevant performance goals whilst Emma was tasked with collecting, checking and accurately summarising data into the weekly report. She was also asked to distribute it by 5pm each Wednesday.

Emma achieved most of this, collecting and including the information she needed in the report in time for the deadline the following week.

However the volume of queries she received about the report demonstrated to both Emma and David that she needed some help to create a clear, concise summary of the data she had collected.

David realises that in the set-up phase he had not discussed how Emma could evaluate the impact of her new report. He recognised that if he had discussed the report compilation and distribution rather than imposing his own solution Emma would have had a better grasp of how to adjust her approach from the outset. He had inadvertently fallen into the age old trap of creating coachee reliance by trying to cut corners at the start of the problem solving process.

Chapter check

What have you learnt from this chapter?

Check your knowledge by answering these questions:

Self assessment questions

1. What are the two types of measures that will help you to build a performance profile of your coachee?
2. What methods are available to collect information about your coachee's current performance?

Chapter 5 – Summary & Actions

In this chapter we recommended that you:

- Draw on a number of sources to identify your coachee's current performance profile.
- Examine both quantitative and qualitative measures of performance to obtain a rounded view of performance.
- Collect data and encourage your coachee to do the same.
- Analyse performance objectively – using indicators such as KPIs to determine whether an individual's current performance standards will enable you to achieve your team's business objectives.

Your action plan

Consider the actions you will take to encourage performance improvement in your team, department or company.

Ask yourself:

- What sources are available to you to analyse performance? Are there any others that you should be using?
- Are you measuring performance from both a quantitative and qualitative perspective?
- How do you encourage your coachees to self assess their performance?
- How do you ensure you are as objective as possible when analysing the performance of your coachees?

Make a note of any aspects that you feel you can improve. Then plan how to address the areas you have identified.

Chapter 6

The C of Procoach

Commit to development

"Commitment is an act, not a word."

JEAN-PAUL SARTRE

C: Commit to development

Key chapter points

- Your aim during this step is to motivate your coachee to make a change in their working practices, and commit to making this change.
- Different coachees will need different types of objectives. Relative experience and capability will mean variations of objectives will be required across your team.
- To achieve the outcomes you wish, consider both results and behaviours during your performance discussion.
- Explore with the coachee the reasons for a performance gap. It may be an ability or motivation issue – or both.
- Agree a suitable approach to address the performance gap, considering whether you are addressing an ability or motivation issue when choosing the approach.
- Help motivate the coachee by asking them to describe an outcome they find inspirational.
- Decide whether you will coach an ability or skill issue yourself – or whether it is more appropriate to involve someone else.

How do you agree performance goals?

You have built a profile of your coachee's current performance and have also encouraged them to examine their working practice. You are now ready to begin a coaching conversation with your coachee.

During your coaching conversation you will:

Objectively explore with your coachee their current performance using the profile you built in Step B

Jointly agree current performance gaps or potential and explore their cause

Agree on development for a specific area where working practice can be improved

Plan how skills practice will take place

Why is Step C important?

Step C is at the heart of effective performance coaching and alongside Step D is where a significant number of the coaching skills you can learn during a Procoach programme are needed.

If you make effective use of the coaching conversation you will have given the coachee the best opportunity to be both motivated to make a difference to their working practice and make a commitment to the specific development you have discussed with them.

Where does Step C fit into the Procoach A-E model?

As you can see from the model's structure, we regard Step C as central to performance coaching.

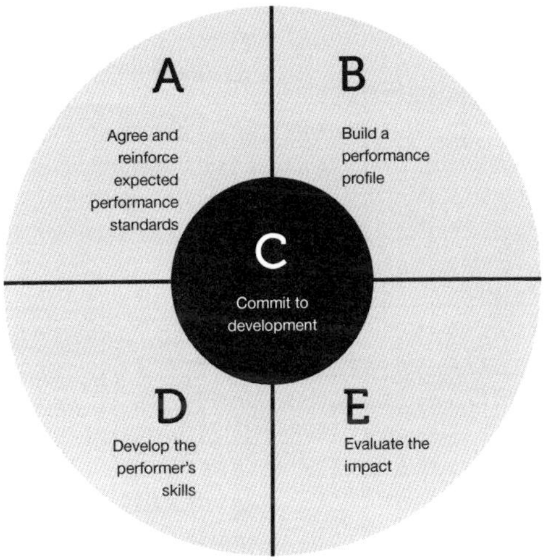

By completing Step C the coachee will have an action plan in line with the standards and performance profile identified and agreed in Steps A and B. At this point you can also check and (if necessary) help the coachee to resolve any motivation or attitude issues that are preventing them from making changes to their skills or knowledge levels.

It is important to note that skill development does not take place during Step C. This is the purpose of Step D, which we describe later.

Explaining Step C

During Step C we identify and agree performance opportunities and how to address these.

The criteria we use during Step C to provide a best practice structure to the coaching conversation is laid out below.

Step C structure and criteria

As with the earlier Steps, these assessment criteria form the basis on which we determine whether a coach has reached our Procoach standard.

Effective delivery of Step C is a combination of the structure shown with the appropriate balance of the behavioural skills.

Use behavioural skills to engage with the coachee

Use the ability / motivation grid to inform your approach

Agree a motivational performance goal and how it will be achieved

Introduction

- Uses ‘small talk’ and non-work topics to put the coachee at ease.
- Explains the purpose of the conversation.
- Explains the process of the conversation.
- Outlines the intended outcomes.
- Seeks agreement with the coachee and permission to proceed.

Body

- Seeks the coachee’s view of performance results and working practice.
- Draws out strengths and then performance gaps.
- Affirms and/or supports the coachee’s view.
- Expands on areas to develop.
- Prompts for omissions by the coachee.
- Agrees a development plan.

Summary

- Restates key areas for development.
- Seeks coachee’s commitment.
- Confirms next steps.

The structure of Introduction, Body and Summary should be upheld and the discussion of strengths should preceed that of development needs. However the precise sequence of some steps needs to be determined by the need for a relaxed and conversational tone to the meeting.

For example you might:

1. Encourage the coachee to discuss development areas at more than one point in the conversation.

2. Ask the coachee to share their views about specific aspects of their performance at several stages of the conversation.

You might find it helpful initially to have this structure to hand so you can check during a coaching conversation that you are including all the relevant elements. The structure will particularly help during your self analysis. Use it to decide whether your coaching helped your coachee to be clear about what they have discussed with you, and how you jointly arrived at conclusions.

Behavioural skills

As outlined in Chapter 3 there are six behavioural skills we recommend as effective in a coaching conversation.

These behavioural skills can be applied to both Steps C and D of the coaching process.

Our 30 years of experience has enabled us to determine the proportions you should expect to see of each behaviour during an effective coaching conversation.

ASKING	Proportion of your conversation
Drawing out	12 - 40%
Confirming	12 - 25%
Challenging	0 - 10%

TELLING	Proportion of your conversation
Supporting	8 - 18%
Guiding	2 - 35%
Releasing tension	0 - 5%

Each coaching conversation will be different, but as a guide, we regard a 3:2 ratio between asking and telling behaviours as an effective balance.

Types of performance objective

As previously mentioned, there are two reasons to set a performance objective:

1. To close the gap between required performance and actual performance.
2. To help a coachee achieve their full potential above and beyond role requirements.

The type of objective you agree will be determined by the nature of development sought.

Performance opportunity	Type of performance objective	Description
Gap	Develop	If an employee's performance is not up to the required standard.
Coachee potential	Maintain	Working with a high performing individual to ensure their high standard of performance is maintained.
	Improve	An 'average' performer who is doing well but not to the standard to which they're capable.

We find that many managers focus on the first two performance areas. However driving improvement with 'average' performers delivers the most significant results in terms of team performance, so should not be overlooked.

Explore performance

Having agreed which aspect of the coachee's performance you wish to discuss, you can explore the coachee's current attainment and which element of working practice they need to adjust.

What makes up performance?

Performance comprises both results (what we want our people to do) and behaviours (the way we want them to do it). You may need to agree both to get the outcomes required.

Results will consist of metrics such as:	**Behaviours include:**
• Achievement of a revenue target. • Delivery of an objective within a defined timeframe. • Meeting deadlines.	• Absenteeism. • Ownership of issues. • Demonstration of company values. • Accuracy. • Articulation. • Adherence to processes.

You need to know how your coachee is currently performing so monitor progress regularly, look for evidence such as the metrics above to form a perspective of their strengths, development needs and consistency. Look for patterns of behaviour over time.

The causes of performance gaps and the opportunity to release coachee potential?

The ability of an individual to deliver the results required of them, or to realise their full potential, can be attributed to four things:

1. Their skills
2. Their knowledge
3. Their mindset
4. The environment and resources available

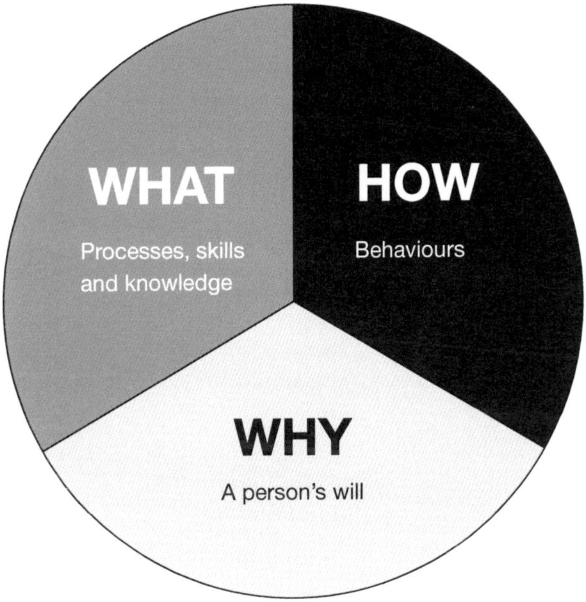

In the coaching conversation, it is the role of the coach to uncover, in association with the coachee, which combination of these factors, when altered, will lead to the realisation of the objectives set.

"Believe in yourself! Have faith in your abilities! Without a humble but reasonable confidence in your own powers you cannot be successful or happy."

NORMAN VINCENT PEALE

A suitable solution for mindset and ability needs

One of the hardest things to determine as a coach is whether a shortfall in performance is due to mindset or skills/knowledge.

The table below provides some questions you can ask yourself to determine whether there is an ability or motivation need – or both.

Ability	Motivation
A **quantitative** measure of knowledge, skills or ability to perform the role	A group of **qualitative** measures and opinions about a person's approach to their role
Questions you would ask yourself:	Questions you would ask yourself:
• Can they meet standards, targets and objectives? • Have they done it before? • How consistently? (etc.)	• How confident are they? • What do others think of them? • Willing to try? (or to change?) • What is their confidence level?

If a lack of motivation or attitude is limiting a coachee's performance then you need to bring this into the open and identify its cause. This should always be resolved before attempting any development of a coachee's ability. In other words, you need to discuss and resolve any opportunities to improve motivation during Step C, before moving onto Step D, where skill coaching takes place.

This approach ensures there is 'ownership' of the need to improve and a willingness to succeed. This also gives you an opportunity to work on or enhance knowledge, skills or ability through development activities.

Techniques to reflect a coachee's ability and motivation

Depending on the level of ability and motivation present, different techniques are suitable. We've suggested four approaches here:

Guide and Lead

Ask yourself:

- How should I use a coachee's motivation to get involved in developing performance related skills?

Release and Delegate

Consider:

- How shall I use a non directive hands-off approach with a focus on the result?
- How shall I question to engage and motivate the learning process?

Direct

- During coaching, the emphasis will be on a more telling style to help the coachee understand what is expected and the end game.
- Use questioning to help understand the motivational blocks and what support is required.

Enthuse and Challenge

- The emphasis is on questioning and challenging supportively to engage the coachee in their development and coaching use.

Motivation

Ability

Case Study

David examines his application of Step C with Emma:

David examines his approach to Step C.

Firstly he assesses the type of performance objective he had agreed with Emma. True, she was struggling to structure her reports clearly, but she had the key skills. So he saw the objective as one of improvement, to address her decreased productivity as a result of the phone calls.

Looking at the two parts of her performance, results and behaviours, David swiftly concluded that Emma's needs related to a skill issue. Emma had proved from her conversations with David that she was very willing to grow and become an increasingly valued team member.

In terms of David's approach to her development areas he considered that his approach to encourage Emma to organise her own development was right. He regarded her ability and motivation as high, she simply needed a few tips from Jan to modify her report writing skills.

In all David concluded, he had provided the right sort of coaching for Emma.

> "The difference between the impossible and the possible lies in a man's determination."
>
> TOMMY LASORDA

DEFINITION

Motivational goals:
A goal that the coachee regards as important.

Motivational goal setting

Once you have identified a performance gap and its cause, you need to agree a goal that the coachee is willing to work towards and achieve.

This is where motivational goals come in. Motivational goals are those that the coachee regards as important.

What type of goal would motivate you?

It is likely that these types of goal would be motivational:

- One you had decided to aim for.
- One that means a lot to you personally.
- One you had committed to, because you wanted the result.

What type of goal may never get reached?

There are many reasons for not achieving goals. Here are a few reasons why this might happen. The goal:

- Was someone else's, provided to you.
- Seems OK, but you lose interest somehow.
- Appears impossible or is unclear, which de-motivates you.

"What lies behind you and what lies in front of you, pales in comparison of what lies inside of you."

RALPH WALDO EMERSON

An "inspirational outcome"

An inspirational outcome is essential to helping the coachee improve their performance. Defining the outcome with your coachee and asking them to put it into their own terms helps them to directly relate to what success feels like.

When working with a coachee to create an inspirational outcome, ask these four questions:

STEP 1

What do you want specifically (a positive statement)?

STEP 2

When, where and with whom do you want it? (timing & context)

STEP 3

Where are you now in respect of the outcome you seek?

STEP 4

What will you be seeing, hearing, and feeling when you get it?

KEY ADVICE

Inspirational outcomes are "well formed".

In other words, they make the goal agreed with the coachee desirable and achievable, by making the goal real to the coachee – and something they connect to kinesthetically.

Planning the skills practice

Although you may not carry out skills practice during Step C, you should discuss and agree with the coachee how this will happen in Step D. This means the coachee has contributed, understands and has agreed to how skills coaching will take place. Having also accepted the area in which to focus their performance development efforts means there is a firm commitment to development.

We regard skills coaching as an essential part of a manager's performance coaching role. This of course is with the caveat that the manager can only expect to provide coaching for skills if they possess a level of knowledge in this area.

KEY ADVICE

A manager can suggest one-to-one and group coaching sessions, when planning skills development.

Group coaching can help if a few people in the team have similar development requirements. It allows the manager to reinforce a consistent, best practice approach across the team.

Choosing when to provide skills coaching directly

It is important to note at this point that we are not looking for the manager to have expertise or a depth of knowledge. In performance coaching situations, the coach simply needs enough knowledge to be in a position to help the coachee improve their skills.

As an example of this, a manager of a sales team should be in a good position to offer performance coaching practice on subjects such as selling and account management skills. They should both know what best practice looks like and at a high level how the team puts these skills into practice.

There will be some skills for which a manager cannot offer direct coaching support. Perhaps the sales manager doesn't know, in sufficient detail, how to use their customer relationship management system to record orders. Or the performance gap or potential might involve skill practice in an area that doesn't directly relate to sales skills.

In this situation, a manager would need to consider who might provide this support. For example, other team members might be better placed to provide coaching practice. Perhaps someone outside the team, within or external to the organisation would be in better position to provide this support. Some development areas might also benefit from self directed learning. Books, journals, white papers and the web offer many support options that might be suitable. Whichever method(s) of coaching support you choose, it is essential to agree an approach that provides the best opportunity to benefit the coachee.

KEY ADVICE

- What you bring to your role as a coach is as important as any coaching process you can learn. Examine your own values and beliefs.
- The coaching principles and A-E model are your guiding frameworks, but be flexible with your options.
- Impromptu coaching is a useful coaching approach. It is a mentality and a way of operating. Coaching is both a planned and impromptu event.
- Use a hands-off approach where possible. Encourage ownership.
- Be aware of your behaviour when you coach, and adjust your style.
- Your coaching results and the payback will come through practice! However only "perfect practice makes perfect" so be honest with yourself when assessing your own performance.

Case Study

David uses the Step C guidelines

David and Emma are meeting for the first time since Emma received some help from Jan to structure her reports more clearly.

David is determined to follow the Step C guidelines to help Emma get the most from their session.

He begins by having a general chat to Emma, allowing her to relax before outlining what he would like to discuss during the meeting and asking for her confirmation that this is what Emma would also like to cover.

They then begin to discuss the report writing skills she has learnt. Emma is very enthusiastic, explaining that Jan gave her some really good, clear guidelines and that her reports had improved significantly as a result. She has noticed that it takes her less time to write each report and the calls have dropped to a manageable level.

David congratulates her and confirms that he has noticed the difference. Her ability to increase her workload is really helping the team.

He then moves on by prompting Emma for other areas where she feels she can improve.

After some hesitation Emma asks if it is possible to attend a Word Processing course.

After some discussion, David gathers that Emma feels that she can increase her productivity further. Emma finds it particularly difficult to format data from different sources into a single document. They discuss the options available and agree that Emma can pick up some of the skills from Jon, another team colleague. With some prompting, Emma suggests that she will set an agenda for Jon, so he can prepare in advance of their session. Then if she requires more advanced skills, they will look into a tailored course, which would address specific areas. David summarises their decisions and actions, checking that Emma is committed to setting up her session with Jon. Emma writes up the summary and they agree a follow up date, to review her progress.

Chapter check

What have you learnt from this chapter?

Check your knowledge by answering these questions:

Self assessment questions

1. What three types of performance objective might you set with your coachee?
2. Which factors contribute to a person's performance?
3. What type of action might be appropriate if a coachee's performance relates to a mindset issue?
4. As a coach, can you adapt your techniques to match the different levels of ability and motivation in your coachee?
5. What are the three main stages of the step C structure?

Chapter 6 – Summary & Actions

In this chapter we recommended the following:

- Motivate your coachee to make a change in their working practices, and commit to making this change, by involving them.
- Agree different types of performance objective to reflect capabilities of the coachee.
- To achieve the outcomes you desire, consider both results and behaviours during your performance discussion.
- Explore with the coachee the reasons for a performance gap. It may be an ability or motivation issue – or both.
- Use a suitable approach to address the performance gap, considering whether you are addressing an ability or motivation issue.
- Motivate the coachee by asking them to describe an outcome that they find inspirational.
- Decide whether you will develop an ability or skill issue yourself, or whether it is more appropriate to involve someone else.

Your action plan

Consider the actions you will take to encourage performance improvement in your team, department or organisation.

Ask yourself:

- How do you currently discuss and agree performance gaps? Are there any aspects that you could improve?
- What objectives do you currently agree with your coachee? Are they suitable for their current performance levels?
- How can you improve your diagnosis and response to an ability or motivation issue?
- Are the goals you set inspirational for your coachee?
- How do you decide on the most appropriate person to address an ability or skill issue?

Make a note of any aspects that you feel you can improve. Then plan how to make a start on the areas you have identified.

Chapter 7

Step D of Procoach: Develop the performer's skills

D: Develop the performer's skills

Key chapter points

- This step concerns addressing a performance gap for skill or knowledge issues.
- Skill coaching should reflect the needs of the coachee, rather than your style of coaching.
- You can address a skill gap during a coaching conversation in which you identify a need, or you may do this on a subsequent occasion.
- Skills or knowledge development can be undertaken with an individual or a small group.

People learn new skills & knowledge in different ways

As you will have gathered by now, as a coach you need to be adaptable, matching your approach to the needs of your coachee.

Step D of the Procoach A-E model is concerned with addressing the performance gaps and coachee potential identified during Step C, the coaching conversation.

As with previous steps, a coach needs to take into account the needs of their coachee, in learning or enhancing a skill. Be aware when developing skills that different people learn in different ways. This means that as a coach you may need to adapt your style. Your aim is to use an approach that will help your coachee become confident and capable in the skill area.

Consider different people in your team. How do you and they learn? Perhaps one of these descriptions fits:

Get stuck into the action!

These people love role plays and "having a go for real".

Think and take it slower.

These people ask to prepare or want to look at some examples first.

Why is Step D important?

For performance coaching in a business environment, we regard it as essential that a manager, can provide ongoing skills practice and feedback in areas where they might reasonably be expected to have some expertise. This is the "What to coach".

This is why we regard Step D as an essential element of effective coaching. We provide guidance through our Procoach programme about the elements that make up successful skill coaching. We often find other performance coaching models do not address this step.

In addition to a manager having an intimate knowledge of how their team operates and how to apply skills, there is another benefit to the manager as a coach, providing skill development during Step D.

This benefit relates to the way in which we learn.

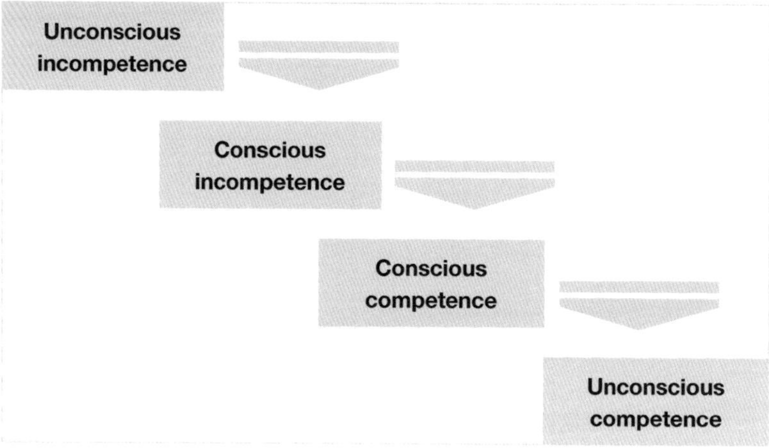

Based on Learning Stages model, Gordon Training International

When learning a new skill, everyone passes through four stages of development, shown above. We progressively become more adept at a skill by constantly reinforcing the use of that skill, through application and receiving feedback.

A manager is available far more often than say a classroom facilitator. They can therefore provide ongoing motivation to continue to apply a newly learnt skill. And they can give constructive feedback about how their team member is applying the skill. This allows the coachee to continuously adapt their application of a skill, until they become unconsciously competent, in other words, they carry out the skill without conscious consideration of their actions.

Where does Step D fit into the Procoach A-E model?

Although this model represents five distinct stages of performance coaching, when you become adept at coaching (i.e. moving towards unconscious competence) you will begin to apply this model more flexibly.

As a coaching novice, it is helpful to learn and apply each step as a distinct stage. You can then begin to apply the steps in a more fluid way, responding as appropriate to coachee's needs.

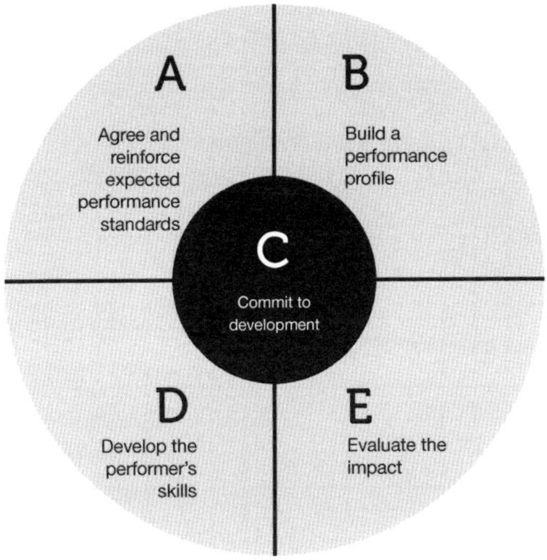

One method of introducing flexibility early in the process of becoming a better coach is to consider how you are using Steps C and D. In some situations, you might find it better to carry out both Steps C and D in a single session, allowing them to overlap.

For example, a team member might approach you to quickly address a specific development gap.

Following an impromptu conversation (Step C), you might identify an area in which you can provide immediate skill development. Provided both you and the coachee have agreed what development is required and you are prepared to provide the development, you can undertake skill development (Step D) immediately.

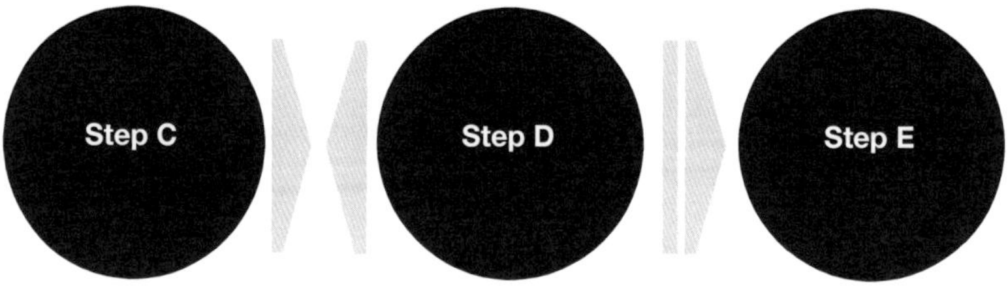

You can then conclude the session once you have achieved the objective. If there are other potential performance gaps and potential that you or the coachee wishes to explore, you could revert to the coaching conversation.

You might also find that for some performance gaps, you do not need to provide skills development. For example, your coachee may have been experiencing a lack of motivation. You would discuss and resolve this with them during Step C. If this is the only reason for their performance gap, there would be no need for skills development.

Step C, then D

This might happen in a single session or separate sessions, depending on what is suitable. (e.g. Step D might need some preparation)

Step C, but no D

You might decide the coachee does not need developmental help or that you cannot provide it personally at that time.

Step C diverting briefly into D

You might decide to validate whether a skill or knowledge gap actually exists.

Your coaching options

As we mentioned in the last section, when discussing your plans for skill coaching you can provide different types of development opportunity.

One-to-one and small group sessions are both useful practice methods. You can also ask a team member or someone outside the team to run a short development session.

Consider online skill development

There are many online resources such as discussion groups, blogs, videos and white papers available too.

Case Study

David considers a recent impromptu coaching session with Emma:

David had just concluded a coaching session with Emma.

It had started as a result of an informal chat when Emma had met David in the corridor. David could tell something was bothering her. When prompted she explained that she was about to make her first presentation to their department and she was nervous.

David suggested they spend a few minutes talking it through. This gave him the opportunity to find out what it was about the presentation that concerned Emma. She explained that she struggled to keep presentations snappy. She often lost her audience as a result. She wanted to make a good first impression, not bore them!

David checked Emma's knowledge of presentation structures and they concluded that her knowledge was good and that a bit of practice might calm her nerves and help her deliver a great presentation. David suggested that Emma bring along the presentation she had prepared so that she could practice with David and he could help her to improve any areas they identified.

Emma and David arranged to meet later that afternoon.

Chapter check

What have you learnt from this chapter?

Check your knowledge by answering these questions:

Self assessment questions

1. What different options are available to provide skills development?
2. How can you use Steps C and D flexibly to suit the coaching need?

Chapter 7 – Summary & Actions

In this chapter we suggested that:

- This step concerns addressing a performance gap for an ability or skill issue.
- Skill development should reflect the needs of the coachee, rather than your style of coaching.
- You may coach to address a skill gap during the session in which you identified the need, or you may do this on a separate occasion.
- Development sessions can be for an individual or a small group.

Your action plan

Consider the actions you will take to encourage performance improvement in your team, department or organisation.

Ask yourself:

- How do you currently coach? Is it in a style that will be most beneficial to your coachee?
- What opportunities do you take to coach in-the-moment? Is this always appropriate? How can you judge this?
- What development sessions have you carried out for an individual, that would benefit your team?

Make a note of any aspects you feel could improve. Then plan how to make a start on the areas you've identified.

Chapter 8

Step E of Procoach: Evaluate the impact

"Quality is never an accident. It is always the result of intelligent effort."

JOHN RUSKIN

E: Evaluate the impact

Key chapter points

- This step is concerned with assessing both the progress of your coachee and your effectiveness as a coach.
- You should evaluate the contribution your coachee makes to business results and how your coaching has influenced this.

Effective coaches look at progress made by their coachee at regular intervals. They compare it to the original development plan to check that the coachee has achieved their objectives.

A second part of this evaluation step involves an assessment of their personal coaching delivery in supporting the coachee.

Your coachee's progress

- Have there been changes in habits, new behaviour and/or different results?
- What qualitative and quantitative evidence is available?

Consider what you want to measure and how you are going to do this.

Your development as a coach – self-assessment

- Be objective about the effectiveness of your coaching.
- Do not be afraid to ask for feedback from others.
- Assess yourself against the five foundations of Procoach.

Having carried out your assessment, consider how your findings will influence your next coaching efforts.

Case Study

David considers his coaching of Emma:

Emma has just completed her departmental presentation and David is pleased to observe that she engaged with her audience, showed few nerves and even managed to make the occasional joke.

He intends to feed this back to Emma after checking how she felt the presentation went. He hopes that she felt as comfortable as she looked.

He also wants to ask her about his coaching. Has it worked for her? He decides that he will ask her to evaluate his coaching approach and suggest any areas he can improve.

Chapter check

What have you learnt from this chapter?

Check your knowledge by answering these questions:

Self assessment questions

1. What two assessments do you need to carry out during Step E of the Procoach A-E approach?
2. What forms of evidence might you look for as part of your evaluation of your coachee's progress?

Chapter 8 – Summary & Actions

In this chapter we covered:

- This step is concerned with regularly assessing both the progress of your coachee and your effectiveness as a coach.
- By assessing both, you can evaluate the contribution your coachee makes to business results and how your coaching has influenced this.

Your action plan

Consider the actions you will take to encourage performance improvement in your team, department or organisation.

Ask yourself:

- How regularly do you assess your coachees' progress?
- How often do you review your performance as a coach? Who do you ask for feedback on your coaching?

Make a note of any aspects that you feel you can improve. Then plan how to work on the areas you've identified.

Overall Summary & Actions

You have now reached the end of our description of our Procoach approach and model. In this book we looked at:

- The rationale and principles behind Prosell's performance coaching approach.
- Two causes of a performance gap or a shortfall in coachee's potential.
- What the Procoach approach aims to achieve.
- The five mindset principles required of a coach.
- The Procoach structure and an in-depth look at the A-E model.

Your action plan

Consider what actions you will take as a result of reading this book.

Ask yourself:

1. What skills and techniques do you need to build, to become an effective performance coach?
2. How close are you to having a coaching mindset? What aspects do you need to work on?
3. Does the coaching model used in your organisation provide your coachees with the support they need to improve their performance?

Make a note of any aspects that you feel you can improve. Then plan how to make a start on the areas you've identified.

"The past cannot be changed. The future is yet in your power."

HUGH WHITE

Conclusions and recommendations

Now that you have reached the end of this book we hope you have a greater insight into performance coaching and how it can make a dramatic difference to business results through improved performance by individuals.

We would suggest that, now you have learnt a little about the power of performance coaching you examine what already exists in your organisation. Then consult this book to decide where any gaps exist in the coaching provision available to you. Finally identify any areas in which you can personally make a difference. For example perhaps you can start to apply some of these concepts with your team.

Good luck with your performance coaching journey!

Additional Information

Research and articles

How can you accurately measure customer satisfaction?

Retentions and referrals are a good measure of business success and suggest you have engaged, motivated employees.

Net promoter scores (NPS) help you to track these over time. Developed by Fred Reichheld and Satmetrix, Bain & Company (Net Promoter, NPS, and Net Promoter Score), they identified through research that the single most important question to ask any customer is whether they would recommend your company to a friend or colleague.

Using a 0 to 10 scale, they divide respondents to this question into three groups:

Response	Customer category
9 or 10	Promoters
7 or 8	Passives
0 - 6	Detractors

NPS Calculation
NPS = Percentage of promotors less percentage of detractors

A good NPS is relative to your market and how your competitors are scoring. As a rule of thumb, Satmetrix provide this guidance:

Company type	NPS
Average	5% – 10%
Most efficient growth engines	50% – 80%

Customers who actively support your brand are more likely to become repeat customers, recommend others (generally at a low acquisition cost), and be less price sensitive. In other words, promoters are sustainably profitable. Detractors, on the other hand, are more likely to shop around, complain to the company and be less profitable.

Sales Executive Council (SEC) report

Performance coaching is about effecting change. It is an approach that helps individuals to enhance their current performance by focusing on the cause of a performance gap or potential rather than the results of the performance – the symptoms.

You can find research into the impact of performance coaching in the business world in the report "Building Solutions-Ready Sales Managers" Sales Executive Council (SEC 2005).

The report supports the conclusion that coaching and mentoring represent one of three elements that separate star managers from an average manager.

The report also looked at the amount of coaching desirable to make a difference to results. The optimum coaching time spent with each coachee averaged out at 3-5 hours per month.

Importantly for business growth, the report found a link between coaching and achievement of sales targets. The research suggested that sales teams with less than two hours coaching a month averaged 90% of target. Those with more than three hours coaching per month averaged 107% of target. Quite a difference and one that suggests performance coaching can produce tangible results.

References

Heskett, J., Jones, T., and Loveman, G. (2008) Putting the Service-Profit Chain to Work. Available at: http://hbr.org/2008/07/putting-the-service-profit-chain-to-work/ar/1

Prosell (2013) Can coaching deliver performance improvement? Available at http://prosell.com/ebook-can-coaching-deliver-performance-improvement

Prosell (2004) Is the UK sales and service line management working? Available at http://prosell.com/resources/search/f8d2e3c597215ae557814079485f991a

Sales Executive Council (SEC) (2005) "Building Solutions-Ready Sales Managers"

Recommended further reading

First Break All The Rules: What The World's Greatest Managers Do Differently
Marcus Buckingham and Curt Coffman
1st edn. Reading:Pocket Books.2005

The Growth Mindset: How You Can Fulfil Your Potential
Dr Carol Dweck
New York: Robinson 2012

Bounce: The Myth Of Talent And The Power Of Practice
Matthew Syed
New York: Fourth Estate 2010

Best Practice in Performance Coaching: A Handbook For Leaders, Coaches, HR Professionals and Organisations
Carol Wilson
London: Kogan Page 2011